Yellow Glove

Books by Naomi Shihab Nye available from Breitenbush:

Different Ways to Pray
1980 Voertman Award, Texas Institute of Letters
$7.00 paper

Hugging the Jukebox
1982 National Poetry Series Winner
1982 Voertman Award, Texas Institute of Letters
1982 Most Notable Books, American Library Assoc.
$7.00 paper

($1.00 postage and handling)

BREITENBUSH BOOKS
BOX 02137
PORTLAND, OR 97202-0137

YELLOW GLOVE

Naomi Shihab Nye

BREITENBUSH **B**OOKS
•Portland/Seattle•

First Edition 2 3 4 5 6 7 8 9

Library of Congress Cataloging in Publication Data

Nye, Naomi Shihab
    Yellow glove.

    I. Title.
PS3564.Y44Y4   1986   811'.54   86-21534
ISBN 0-932576-41-9
ISBN 0-932576-42-7 (pbk.)

Publication of this book is made possible, in part, by a grant from the National Endowment for the Arts, a federal agency, to whom the author and publisher express their sincere gratitude.

Text and cover design by Patrick Ames.
The typeface is Palatino. Composition by Seattle ImageSetting.

Breitenbush Books are published by James Anderson.
Breitenbush Books, Box 02137, Portland, OR 97202-0137

Manufactured in the U.S.A. by McNaughton & Gunn, Ann Arbor, MI.

The author is grateful to the editors of the following for permission to reprint poems that appeared earlier in:

The Georgia Review, Quarry West, The Madison Review, The Bloomsbury Review, The Chowder Review, Amphora Review, Domestic Crude, The Midwest Quarterly, Third Woman, Trinity Review, Pax, Telescope, Painted Bride Quarterly, Tarasque, Forum, Scape, Christian Century, The Christian Science Monitor, Cedar Rock, Ariel, Aileron, Approach, The Muslim, 2 Plus 2

And also in the following anthologies:
The Pushcart Prize IX, The Morrow Anthology of Younger American Poets, New American Poets of the 80s, Pangaea, Kinverse, And Not Surrender.

"The Use of Fiction" first appeared in *Antaeus.*

"Catalogue Army" and "The Man Who Hated Trees" first appeared in *Poetry.*

"Looking for the Cat Grave" first appeared in *The Kenyon Review.*

"Office 337, Wheeler Hall, Berkeley," "Telling the Story," and "No One Thinks of Tegucigalpa" first appeared in *Prairie Schooner.*

"Arabic Coffee" first appeared as a broadside from Iguana Press.

Special thanks to the Na-Bolom Community, San Cristobal de las Casas, Chiapas, Mexico.

For Madison Cloudfeather

CONTENTS

TRYING TO NAME WHAT DOESN'T CHANGE

Roselva says the only thing that doesn't change
is train tracks. She's sure of it.
The train changes, or the weeds that grow up spidery
by the side, but not the tracks.
I've watched one for three years, she says,
and it doesn't curve, doesn't break, doesn't grow.

Peter isn't sure. He saw an abandoned track
near Sabinas, Mexico, and says a track without a train
is a changed track. The metal wasn't shiny anymore.
The wood was split and some of the ties were gone.

Every Tuesday on Morales Street
butchers crack the necks of a hundred hens.
The widow in the tilted house
spices her soup with cinnamon.
Ask her what doesn't change.

Stars explode.
The rose curls up as if there is fire in the petals.
The cat who knew me is buried under the bush.

The train whistle still wails its ancient sound
but when it goes away, shrinking back
from the walls of the brain,
it takes something different with it every time.

HELLO

Some nights
the rat with pointed teeth
makes his long way back
to the bowl of peaches.
He stands on the dining room table
sinking his tooth
drinking the pulp
of each fruity turned-up face
knowing you will read
this message and scream.
It is his only text,
to take and take in darkness,
to be gone before you awaken
and your giant feet
start creaking the floor.

Where is the mother of the rat?
The father, the shredded nest,
which breath were we taking
when the rat was born,
when he lifted his shivering snout
to rafter and rivet and stone?
I gave him the names of the devil,
seared and screeching names,
I would not enter those rooms
without a stick to guide me,
I leaned on the light, shuddering,
and the moist earth under the house,
the trailing tails of clouds,
said he was in the closet,
the drawer of candles,
his nose was a wick.

How would we live together
with our sad shoes and hideouts,
our lock on the door

and his delicate fingered paws
that could clutch and grip,
his blank slate of fur
and the pillow where we press our faces?
The bed that was a boat is sinking.
And the shores of morning loom up
lined with little shadows,
things we never wanted to be, or meet,
and all the rats are waving hello.

THE GARDENER

Everything she planted gave up under the ground.
That's how it was in some lives; dig a little hole,
drop the seed, and forget it.

Each morning she woke early,
scouted the numb corners of her house
untangling rooms.
The brimming rooster seemed sure of the day.
Down the block, the house of screaming women
was quiet now, lost in its own startled breath.

In morning sentences began again:
Solomon Henry jogging past
with shopping bags and ragged lungs
might have a new answer for *Doin' okay?*

Almost ruined, he'd say.
Some month, year, he might pause,
raise the bags high over his head.
"I found it," he'd announce.
"And it was a bargain too."

You learned which stories needed help
to make them bearable. The furious wife
with seventeen dogs stirring cocoa
in her wrecked kitchen, saying Sit down,
Solomon, the boy running from the screamers' house
with hands over ears and eyes closed. . .
maybe he'd inherit their old farm when they died.
Maybe the clear air could rebuild his memory.

Maybe the seeds were waiting, hibernating,
so an unexpected larkspur or celery
would poke its thin shoot out of the earth

and be part of the story in a new place,
be a completely different character
than it would have been had it come up
on schedule. Excellent for bordering
said the package. Splendid color profusion.
It did not say, you will wait and wait
for a reason.
You will bend, looking.
You will want to blame every worm.

OFFICE 337, WHEELER HALL, BERKELEY

I live in a room of abandoned things,
typewriters with jammed ribbons,
clocks that won't wind.
Shelves of books inscribed,
"To Clark, with respect and good wishes."
Clark has moved to another building
without them.

Each day students weave stories
beneath my window.
A boy asks a girl if her interest in him
is growing, and she says, "No."
He should come up and sit
in my office awhile.
Here he could learn what it is to be
a green vinyl chair losing its stuffing.

I like this room so much
I fling the window high
to let the sky in.
Join me, I say.
Whatever leaves us
leaves us both.
I open the door of my heart
so the losses march out.
Now when the call comes
saying my tricky cat is dead,
when the fuschia blossoms
make pink tombs in the grass,
a question I asked years ago
is being answered.

Today a gray nest
fell out of a spruce at my feet.
I lifted it, traced the hollow

where a bird once sat,
and looked up.
The tree was very tall.

I brought the nest to my office,
circled it with eucalyptus leaves
that had also fallen,
fragrant grace notes—
I buried my face
in this shrine of knitted twigs
and sang the song
to all things that are gone:
Tu-ra-lu-ra-lu-ra,
it says, you make a short time
seem long.

NEW YEAR

Maybe the street is tired of being a street.
They tell how it used to be called Bois d'Arc,
now called Main, how boys in short pants
caught crawdads for supper at a stone acequia
now covered over.
Sometimes the street sweeper stops his machine
and covers his eyes.

Think of the jobs people have.
The girl weighing citron in the basement
of H.L. Green's, for a man who says
he can't wait to make fruitcake
and she says, What is this stuff anyway
before it looks like this? and he leaves
on his cane, slowly, clutching the bag.
Then she weighs garlics for a trucker.

Think of the streams of headlights
on the Houston freeway all headed somewhere
and where they will be headed after that.
After so long, even jets might be tired of acceleration,
slow-down, touching-ground-again,
as a child is so tired of his notebook
he pastes dinosaurs on it to render it extinct.
Or the teacher, tired of questions,
hearing the anthem *How long does it have to be?*
play itself over and over in her sleep
and she just doesn't know. As long as you want it.

What was this world? Where things you never did
felt more real than what happened.
Your friend's dishtowel strung over her faucet

was a sentence which could be diagrammed
while your tumbled life, that basket of phrases,
had too many ways it might fit together.

Where a street might just as easily have been
a hair ribbon in a girl's ponytail
her first day of dance class, teacher in mauve leotard
rising to say, We have much ahead of us,
and the little girls following, kick, kick, kick,
thinking what a proud sleek person she was,
how they wanted to be like her someday,
while she stared outside the window at the high wires
strung with ice, the voices inside them opening out
to every future which was not hers.

THE TUNNEL OF QUESTIONS

What's been going on?
Gene asked Rusty at the reunion.
Rusty answered, I'm sorry sir,
but you'll have to be more specific,
which made the sky between us light up
like the best answer lights the mouth
of the boy who speaks it. His classmates
stare in awe. How did he know?
We cannot say what is going on,
or what we want to be when we grow up,
just as we cannot grow up.

I held rupees in my hand.
The Abu Dhabi airport is shaped like a mushroom.
He purchased a house with thick stone walls.
All the time my friend was dying,
she said a carved owl spoke to her.
The last letter—"I still have hope,
that's something you don't lose"—
has burrowed a tunnel inside my throat.
Questions live there. As for hope,
something inside us is a stone
bigger than moving, and the question is
how to love it.

Last summer a bull escaped from the stockyards,
clattered down Main Street looking for grass.
He found some. Bounded away again when the truck came
with pistols and nets, and all the old men
who pass by draping beat-up coats over their arms,
lugging sacks of crushed soda cans,
felt a little cry come out of their own tunnels

when the truck caught up with the bull
on the Salvation Army steps.
He didn't get away.
Could he have gotten away?

The days which are brothers to us
pump their blood back and forth,
not telling. A man crosses a street,
using his shadow as an oar. And still
we want to go places, saying
if we lived in Portugal, we could eat
white beans and shrimp,
bury our faces in vats of orange petals.
Or Paris—visiting the flower market
every day might change things,
the questions grow different bodies,
fluting out of themselves into yellow crowns
on slim green stalks. And the days you felt
the questions open into boats
and drift, leaving you
like some bridge or umbrella-table, firm?
That was the day you walked
like a free man or woman nodding your head
and said whatever had to be done,
you could do it.

STREETS

A man leaves the world
and the streets he lived on
grow a little shorter.

One more window dark
in this city, the figs on his branches
will soften for birds.

If we stand quietly enough evenings
there grows a whole company of us
standing quietly together.
Overhead loud grackles are claiming their trees
and the sky which sews and sews, tirelessly sewing,
drops her purple hem.
Each thing in its time, in its place,
it would be nice to think the same about people.

Some people do. They sleep completely,
waking refreshed. Others live in two worlds,
the lost and remembered.
They sleep twice, once for the one who is gone,
once for themselves. They dream thickly,
dream double, they wake from a dream
into another one, they walk the short streets
calling out names, and then they answer.

THE HOUSE IN THE HEART

How it is possible to wake this empty
and brew chamomile, watching the water
paint itself yellow and the little flowers
float and bob—

The cars swishing past in dark rain
are going somewhere.
This is my favorite story.
The man with a secret jungle growing
in his brain says chocolate
can make him happy.
I would find a bar
heavy as a brick. With almonds.
And lean forward whispering of
the house in the heart,
the one with penny-size rooms,
moth-wing ceilings, cat-lip doors.

This body we thought so important,
it's a porch, that's all.
I know this, but I don't know
what to do about it.

How it is possible to move
through your own kitchen
touching a bamboo strainer curiously:
Whose is this? And know it is
the one you use every tea,
to feel like an envelope
that travels in and out of the world
carrying messages
and yet not remember
a single one of them—

Today I look out the glass
for some confirmation.
The lights will stay on late this morning.
Palm tree fronds were frozen last week,
there is rain in the street.
And the house in the heart cries
no one home, no one home.

OLD IRON

Some days the words pass us,
cars loaded with vacationers.
We are not going where they are going.
Soon as they top the hill
we'll be on the lost road again,
shouting once, then listening,
kicking a stone toward
anything like a tree.

Then the first language crawls back
into the ears, humming.
A twig scratches two words
in damp red earth:
NO   THOUGHT.
I'm looking for cedar stumps,
a black calf in a blue field,
anything to report
that has nothing to do with my life.

I'm looking for the rusted skillet
hunters left hanging on a branch.
Years after they sighed in firelight
the tree claims their old iron
as another natural arm.

THE WHITE ROAD

I can't even count
how many of my own feet
walk the white stone road today.
As if the feet of past years
tramped alongside,
and the future feet,
anchors already forming
in the sea of blood,
accompanied.
Why should such a simple sadness
well up like a crowd?

Now I've even forgotten
whose sadness it was to begin with.
Maybe it belongs to the nun
who waits for the 6 A.M. bus,
whose headscarf is white
and always tied.
Maybe she feels lighter today
having dropped it.
Or the man at the state hospital
who kept singing
"These are a few of my favorite things"
though his cigarette trembled
and he wore pajamas in the afternoon—

These stones have smooth backs.
They could be praying, or sleeping.
I could be anyone else,
researching sadness,
finding out how it adheres to the world,
bubbling and thickening, flour in broth,
how women who have lost children
sometimes feel like women
who have lost homes in fires
or men in their fifties who feel
the days shrinking in front of them
sometimes weep for a neighbor boy's dog.

DEW

A Kickapoo grandmother pulled
deerhide moccasins out of her bosom,
said, If you really want these
to fit your feet,
walk in the dew a little,
walk in the dew.

She lived in a cattail hut
ringed by mountains.
There was no road to her house.

I think of her every day
as I touch the forks and curtains,
the pens and melons
that line this life,
feeling how we grow together,
things and the life beyond things,
one gradually fitted motion
moving home across the grass.

SPRUCE STREET, BERKELEY

If a street is named for a tree,
it is right that flowers
bloom purple and feel like cats,
that people are leaves drifting
downhill in morning fog.

Everyone came outside to see
the moon setting like a perfect
orange mouth tipped up to heaven.

Now the cars sleep against curbs.
If I write a letter,
how will I make it long enough?

There is a place to stand
where you can see so many lights
you forget you are one of them.

LOOKING FOR THE CAT GRAVE

1.

Sunlight stripes a wall.
Silent pumpkin sleeps in a river of sun.
Some moments we have spent
our whole lives walking towards.

2.

Dry grass, earth whiskers,
red sweater snagged in a tree.
Being alive is a common road,
it's what we notice makes us different.
A birdhouse becomes a floodlight.
Girls sit in a circle, learning each other
like words to be spoken in lonely places.

3.

I wish this could last. I wish we could stay outside,
sun on our cheeks, a distant engine's roar, forever.
I wish I could remember people's faces
as well as I remember my dead cat's eyes.

THE USE OF FICTION

A boy claims he saw you on a bicycle last week,
touring his neighborhood. "West Cypress Street!" he shouts,
as if your being there and his seeing you
were some sort of benediction.
To be alive, to be standing outside
on a tender February evening . . .
"It was a blue bicycle, ma'am, your braid was flying,
I said hello and you laughed, remember?"

You almost tell him your bicycle seat is thick with dust,
the tires have been flat for months.
But his face, that radiant flower, says you are his friend,
he has told his mother your name.
Maybe this is a clear marble
he will hide in his sock drawer for months.
So who now, in a universe of figures,
would deny West Cypress Street,
throwing up clouds into this literal sky?
"Yes, amigo"—hand on shoulder—
"It was I."

THE SPACIOUS AIR

"A famous myth says that at first the sky was low down, but people became too
familiar with it, and when a woman hit it in the eye with a long pestle the sky
retired in anger to the distance where it has been ever since."

African Mythology

Air gathers words in its wide hands,
returning them later as cloud,
vapor from a cup of tea.
What we said on the road to Abilene
came back later in Alpine,
twisted with a knot of sky.
"I like stories centered on houses, land,"
you said, then told one, a woman
with a shock of yellow hair who lost everything
fifteen times. And went mad, or went
to live by the sea, I can't remember
the ending. What stays with me
is how you said she smiled,
shadow of a sun that hurts to look at.
We were just past the gas station
in the crossroads town where a man claimed,
"I ain't been anywhere in 30 years,"
then filled us up, and it was his smile too,
the same smile a blade has,
spinning in the wind.

In Alpine the chili peppers have hardened
on the branch. We saw fall, winter, they say.
They wait beyond readiness, but something
remains. Air making its own secret harvest.
And the reason grief seems so close on this road
belongs to the rock seller who folded
paper baskets for each agate and apache tear,
saying their names till his tongue was onyx too.
Each one labeled neatly, then he sold
the whole collection, put a gun to his head.
And a word entered the long pause of desert,
silence that slept in the cracks of his walls
became its own basket, one flap over another,
and all this sky inside.

MOON TRIO

1.

Moon of silence, unexpected visitor.
Quickly I leave what I was doing.
Half-sentences roll back into themselves like drawers.
I will give you the smoothest pillow,
the blue glass from Mexico which certain light
can change to sky.

2.

A man from the Zuni reservation
makes parties for the full moon.
He toasts the glowing mesa,
friends arrive and orbit the floor.

Here's one party where the honored guest
brings the gift.

3.

Alfredo in red socks
under a sliver of moon
is doing his job, occupying steps.
For years he has said, "Could be better,
could be worse."
Tonight he is quiet, cigarette
balanced on his lips.
His friend Maria, More-Than-99, babbles
excitedly in Spanish, her white nightgown
billowing out around her as if she were swimming
and the air held it up.

Moon topping the chimney.

Maria, More-Than-99, says,
"We will paint this house."

DEFINING WHITE

On the telephone no one knows what white is.
My husband knows, he takes pictures.
He has whole notebooks defining
how white is white, is black,
and all the gray neighborhoods in between.

The telephone is blind.
Cream-white? Off-white?
I want a white, he says,
that is white-white,
that tends in no direction
other than itself.

Now this is getting complex.
Every white I see is tending
toward something else.
The house was white, but it is peeling.
People are none of these colors.

In the sky white sentences form and detach.
Who speaks here? What breath
scrawls itself endlessly,
white on white, without being heard?
Is wind a noun or a verb?

SURE

Today you rain on me from every corner of the sky
Softly vanishing hair, a tiny tea set from Mexico
perched on a shelf with the life-size cups.

I remember knotting my braid on your bed,
ten months into your silence.
Someone said you were unreachable,
we could chatter and you wouldn't know.
You raised yourself on magnificent dying elbows
to speak one line,
"Don't—be—so—sure."
The room was stunned.
Lying back on your pillow, you smiled at me.
No one else saw it.
Later they even denied they heard.

All your life, never mind.
It hurts, but never mind.
You fed me corn from cans, stirring busily.
I lined up the salt shakers on your table.
We were proud of each other for nothing.
You, because I finished my meal.
Me, because you wore a flowered dress.
Life was a tablet of small reasons.
"That's that," you'd say, pushing back your chair.
"And now let's go see if the bakery has a cake."

Today, as I knelt to spell a word for a little boy,
it was your old floor under me,
cool sections of black and white tile,
I'd lie on my belly tracing their sides.
St. Louis, movies sold popcorn,
baby lions born in zoos,
the newspapers would never find us.

One moth lighting on the sink
in a dark apartment years ago.
You point, should I catch it?
Oh, never mind.
A million motions later, I open my hand,
and it is there.

GOING FOR PEACHES, FREDERICKSBURG, TEXAS

Those with experience look for a special kind.
Red Globe, the skin slips off like a fine silk camisole.
Boy breaks one open with his hands. Yes it's good,
my old relatives say, but we'll look around.
They want me to stop at every peach stand
between Stonewall and Fredericksburg,
leave the air conditioner running,
jump out and ask the price.

Coming up here they talked about
the best ways to die. One favors a plane crash,
but not over a city. One wants to make sure
her grass is watered when she goes.
Ladies, ladies! This peach is fine,
it blushes on both sides.
But they want to keep driving.

In Fredericksburg the houses are stone,
they remind me of wristwatches, glass polished,
years ticking by in each wall.
I don't like stone, says one. What if it fell?
I don't like Fredericksburg, says the other.
Too many Germans driving too slow.
She herself is German as Stuttgart.
The day presses forward, wearing complaints
like charms on its bony wrist.

Actually ladies, (I can't resist),
I don't think you wanted peaches after all,
you just wanted a nip of scenery,
some hills to tuck behind your heads.
The buying starts immediately, from a scarfed woman
who says she gave up teachin' for peachin'.
She has us sign a guest book.
One aunt insists on reloading into her box

to see the fruit on the bottom.
One rejects any slight bruise.
But Ma'am, the seller insists, nature isn't perfect.
Her hands are spotted, like a peach.

On the road, cars weave loose patterns between lanes.
We will float in flowery peach-smell
back to our separate kettles, our private tables
and knives, and line up the bounty,
deciding which ones go where.
A canned peach, says one aunt, lasts ten years.
She was 87 last week. But a frozen peach
tastes better on ice cream.
Everything we have learned so far,
skins alive and ripening, on a day
that was real to us, that was summer,
motion going out and memory coming in.

BREAKING MY FAVORITE BOWL

Some afternoons
thud unexpectedly
and split into four pieces
on the floor.

Two large pieces, two small ones.
I could glue them back,
but what would I use them for?

Forgive me when I answer you
in a voice so swollen
it won't fit your ears.

I'm thinking about apples and histories,
the hands I broke off
my mother's praying statue
when I was four—
how she tearfully repaired them,
but the hairline cracks
in the wrists
were all she said
she could see—

the unannounced blur
of something passing
out of a life.

THE THINLY FLUTED WINGS OF STAMPS

Birds spoke your language by coming to the sill.
Letters cooperated by flying away.
You tore white strips from the hearts of loaves.

The birds were nouns, you could say,
"I saw three gnat-catchers, seventeen cardinals,"
and make a place in the air that was yours.
They brought you whatever their feet had touched,
branch, birdbath, red interlocking roof,
and all the words that mean flight:
dodge, glide, soar.
Fifteen years you nested in one room,
one fluffy pink sweater, without coming downstairs.

I laughed at your letters. "Prince Charles
is still available. Satan sleeps in the White House,
please write back soon." I still laugh.
You were the only person I knew who used real ink.

At night you wondered where the birds were sleeping,
felt their small breath hovering in your bones and hair.
You dreamed your clock became an onion
and sprouted one green shoot.
You were hungry, but wouldn't cut it.
Once I visited you and curtains were flapping,
the sky had eyes. "They need me. The birds need me."
A truck from the bakery delivered twenty loaves.
Every day? You nodded. You said we all had our jobs.

Now I feel your small flights nudging me.
A hundred blackbirds fly north, toward Chicago.
I think maybe they knew you and stand still for a moment,
staring up. This is our ongoing correspondence,
the wing between our worlds: to stoop for small things,
scatter seed for hens, notice the feather has two sides.
There are crazier ways. *Prince Charles taken.*
I lined six stones in the sill and have been watching them
for days.

YELLOW GLOVE

What can a yellow glove mean in a world of motorcars and
governments?

I was small, like everyone. Life was a string of precautions: Don't
kiss the squirrel before you bury him, don't suck candy, pop balloons,
drop watermelons, watch TV. When the new gloves appeared one
Christmas, tucked in soft tissue, I heard it trailing me: Don't lose
the yellow gloves.

I was small, there was too much to remember. One day, waving at a
stream—the ice had cracked, winter chipping down, soon we would
sail boats and roll into ditches—I let a glove go. Into the stream,
sucked under the street. Since when did streets have mouths?
I walked home on a desperate road. Gloves cost money. We didn't
have much. I would tell no one. I would wear the yellow glove that
was left and keep the other hand in a pocket. I knew my mother's
eyes had tears they had not cried yet and I didn't want to be the one
to make them flow. It was the prayer I spoke secretly, folding socks,
lining up donkeys in windowsills. I would be good, a promise made to
the roaches who scouted my closet at night. If you don't get in my
bed, I will be good. And they listened. I had a lot to fulfill.

The months rolled down like towels out of a machine. I sang and
drew and fattened the cat. Don't scream, don't lie, don't cheat, don't
fight—you could hear it anywhere. A pebble could show you how to
be smooth, tell the truth. A field could show how to sleep without
walls. A stream could remember how to drift and change—the next
June I was stirring the stream like a soup, telling my brother dinner
would be ready if he'd only hurry up with the bread, when I saw it.
The yellow glove draped on a twig. A muddy survivor. A quiet flag.

Where had it been in the three gone months? I could wash it, fold it in my winter drawer with its sister, no one in that world would ever know. There were miracles on Harvey Street. Children walked home in yellow light. Trees were reborn and gloves traveled far, but returned. A thousand miles later, what can a yellow glove mean in a world of bankbooks and stereos?

Part of the difference between floating and going down.

THE BRICK

For David and Barbara Clewell

Each morning in the gray margin
between sleep and rising, I find myself
on Pershing Avenue, St. Louis, examining bricks
in buildings, looking for the one I brushed
with my mitten in 1956. How will I know it
when I find it? A shade goes up in one window.
This is where the man in the undershirt lived.
Someone shakes a coffee can and turns a faucet;
the water gushes out, ice-cold.
Why do I want this brick? What does a brick,
red or otherwise, have to tell anyone
about how to live a life? It's as crazy
as crying for a bear when you were three,
those little hands hopefully touching the nose,
maybe they even named it. "Fuzzy."
So what could I name a brick? Hard.
What Buildings Are Made Of.
And why would one brick that I brushed
while on a walk with my mother and father
become a shrine? Later we rode a bus.
My father carried a sack from a drugstore.
I stared hard at the faces of shops
to see what they looked like in the dark.
And things went on that way for decades,
doors opening, buzzers going off,
someone saying, "We're almost there."

So. This has something to do with why
I stare at certain buildings in any city.
I don't know where the mittens went,
they had a cord to keep them together.
I'm sure my parents could drive down
Pershing Avenue tomorrow without weeping.
But it's different for me.
It's the snagged edge, the center of memory,
the place where I get off and on.

BLOOD

"A true Arab knows how to catch a fly in his hands,"
my father would say. And he'd prove it,
cupping the buzzer instantly
while the host with the swatter stared.

In the spring our palms peeled like snakes.
True Arabs believed watermelon could heal fifty ways.
I changed these to fit the occasion.

Years before, a girl knocked,
wanted to see the Arab.
I said we didn't have one.
After that, my father told me who he was,
"Shihab"—"shooting star"—
a good name, borrowed from the sky.
Once I said, "When we die, we give it back?"
He said that's what a true Arab would say.

Today the headlines clot in my blood.
A little Palestinian dangles a truck on the front page.
Homeless fig, this tragedy with a terrible root
is too big for us. What flag can we wave?
I wave the flag of stone and seed,
table mat stitched in blue.

I call my father, we talk around the news.
It is too much for him,
neither of his two languages can reach it.
I drive into the country to find sheep, cows,
to plead with the air:
Who calls anyone *civilized?*
Where can the crying heart graze?
What does a true Arab do now?

LUNCH IN NABLUS CITY PARK

When you lunch in a town which has recently known war
under a calm slate sky mirroring none of it,
certain words feel impossible in the mouth.
Casualty: too casual, it must be changed.
A short man stacks mounds of pita bread
on each end of the table, muttering
something about more to come.
Plump birds landing on park benches
surely had their eyes closed recently,
must have seen nothing of weapons or blockades.
When the woman across from you whispers
I don't think we can take it anymore
and you say there are people praying for her
in the mountains of Himalaya and she says
Lady, it is not enough, then what?

A plate of cigar-shaped meatballs, dish of tomato,
friends dipping bread—
I will not marry till there is true love, says one,
throwing back her cascade of perfumed hair.
He says the University of Texas seems remote to him
as Mars, and last month he stayed in his house
for 26 days. He will not leave, he refuses to leave.
In the market they are selling
men's shoes with air vents, a beggar displays
the giant scab of leg he must drag from alley to alley,
and students gather to discuss what constitutes
genuine protest.

In summers, this cafe is full.
Today only our table sends laughter into the trees.
What cannot be answered checkers the tablecloth
between the squares of white and red.
Where do the souls of hills hide
when there is shooting in the valleys?
What makes a man with a gun seem bigger

than a man with almonds? How can there be war
and the next day eating, a man stacking plates
on the curl of his arm, a table of people
toasting one another in languages of grace:
For you who came so far;
For you who held out, wearing a black scarf
to signify grief;
For you who believe true love can find you
amidst this atlas of tears linking one town
to its own memory of mortar,
when it was still a dream to be built
and people moved here, believing,
and someone with sky and birds in his heart
said this would be a good place for a park.

THE GARDEN OF ABU MAHMOUD

West Bank

He had lived in Spain
so we stood under a glossy loquat tree
telling of madres y milagros
with clumsy tongues.
It seemed strange in the mouth
of this Arab, but no more so
than everything.
Across his valley the military
settlement gleamed white.
He said, That's where the guns live,
as simply as saying, it needs sun,
a plant needs sun.
He stooped to unsheathe an eggplant
from its nest of leaves,
purple shining globe,
and pressed it on me.
I said No, no, I don't want
to take things before they are ripe,
but it was started already,
handfuls of marble-sized peaches,
hard green mish-mish and delicate lilt
of beans. Each pocket swelled
while he breathed mint leaves,
bit the jagged edge.
He said every morning found him here,
before the water boiled on the flame
he came out to this garden,
dug hands into earth saying, I know you
and earth crumbled rich layers
and this result of their knowing—
a hillside in which no inch went unsung.
His enormous onions held light
and the trees so weighted with fruits
he tied the branches up.
And he called it querido, corazon,
all the words of any language
connecting to the deep place
of darkness and seed. He called it
ya habibi in Arabic, my darling tomato,
and it called him governor, king,
and some days he wore no shoes.

34

JERUSALEM

Two girls danced, red flames winding.
I offered my shoes to the gypsies,
threw back my head, and yelled.

All day their hillocks of cheese
had been drying on a goat hide
stretched in the sun.
So it was true—they came in the night,
they set their dark tents flapping.
Gypsies see right through you,
I'd heard a man say in town.
And did they like what they saw?

To live without roads seemed one way
not to get lost. To make maps
of stone and grass, to rub stars together
and find a spark.

I gave American shoes, sandals from Greece.
They held each one curiously, shy to put them on.
Later the shoes disappeared into the tent
and I walked home with their drums in my belly.
Maybe they would use them like vases,
drawers. At least there were choices,
not like a sword, which did only one thing,
or a house, which sat and sat in the desert
after the goats and music had blown away.

THE MAN WHO MAKES BROOMS

So you come with these maps in your head
and I come with voices chiding me to
"speak for my people"
and we march around like guardians of memory
till we find the man on the short stool
who makes brooms.

Thumb over thumb, straw over straw,
he will not look at us.
In his stony corner there is barely room
for baskets and thread,
much less the weight of our faces
staring at him from the street.
What he has lost or not lost is his secret.

You say he is like all the men,
the man who sells pistachios,
the man who rolls the rugs.
Older now, you find holiness in anything
that continues, dream after dream.
I say he is like nobody,
the pink seam he weaves
across the flat golden face of this broom
is its own shrine, and forget about the tears.

In the village the uncles will raise their *kefiyahs*
from dominoes to say, no brooms in America?
And the girls who stoop to sweep the courtyard
will stop for a moment and cock their heads.
It is a little song, this thumb over thumb,
but sometimes when you wait years
for the air to break open
and sense to fall out,
it may be the only one.

Jerusalem, 1983

MY UNCLE MOHAMMED AT MECCA, 1981

This year the wheels of cars
are stronger than the wheels of prayer.
Where were you standing when it hit you,
what blue dome rose up in your heart?

I hold the birds you sent me,
olive wood clumsily carved.
The only thing I have
that you touched.

Why is it so many singulars
attend your name? You lived on one mountain,
sent one gift. You went on one journey
and didn't come home.

We search for the verb
that keeps a man complete.
To resign, to disappear, that's how
I've explained you.

Now I want to believe it was true.
Because you lived apart,
we hold you up. Because no word connected us,
we complete your sentence.

And the house with wind in the windows
instead of curtains
is the house we are building
in the cities of the world.

Uncle of sadness, this is the last pretense:
you understood the world was no pilgrim,
and were brave, and wise,
and wanted to die.

MOTHER OF NOTHING

Sister, the stars have no children.
The stars pecking at each night's darkness
above your trailer would shine back at themselves
in its metal, but they are too far away.
The stones lining your path to the goats
know themselves only as speechless, flat,
gray-in-the-sun.
What begins and ends in the self
without continuance in any other.

You who stand at preschool fences
watching the endless tumble and slide,
who answer the mothers' Which one is yours?
with blotted murmur and turning away,
listen. Any lack carried
too close to the heart
grows teeth, nibbles off
corners. I heard one say
she had no talent,
another, no time, and there were many
without beauty all those years,
and all of them shrinking.
What sinks to the bottom of the pond
comes up with new colors, or not at all.

We sank, and there was purple,
voluptuous merging of purple and blue,
a new silence living
in the houses of our bodies.
Those who wanted and never received;
who were born without hands,
who had and then lost; the Turkish mother
after the earthquake
with five silent children lined before her,

the women of Beirut
bearing water to their bombed-out rooms,
the fathers in offices
with framed photographs of children on their desks,
and their own private knowledge
of all the hard words.

And we held trees differently
then, and dried plates differently,
because waiting dulls the senses
and when you are no longer waiting,
something wakes up. My cousin said
It's not children, it's a matter of making
life. And I saw the streets opening into the future,
cars passing, mothers with car seats,
children waving out the rear window,
keeping count of all who waved back,
and would we lift our hearts and answer them,
and when we did, what would we say?
And the old preposterous stories of nothing
and everything finally equalling one another
returned in the night. And like relatives,
knew where the secret key was hidden
and let themselves in.

ARABIC COFFEE

It was never too strong for us:
make it blacker, Papa,
thick in the bottom,
tell again how the years will gather
in small white cups,
how luck lives in a spot of grounds.

Leaning over the stove, he let it
boil to the top, and down again.
Two times. No sugar in his pot.
And the place where men and women
break off from one another
was not present in that room.
The hundred disappointments,
fire swallowing olive-wood beads
at the warehouse, and the dreams
tucked like pocket handkerchiefs
into each day, took their places
on the table, near the half-empty
dish of corn. And none was
more important than the others,
and all were guests. When
he carried the tray into the room,
high and balanced in his hands,
it was an offering to all of them,
stay, be seated, follow the talk
wherever it goes. The coffee was
the center of the flower.
Like clothes on a line saying
you will live long enough to wear me,
a motion of faith. There is this,
and there is more.

THE TRAVELING ONION

"It is believed that the onion originally came from India. In Egypt it was an object of worship—why I haven't been able to find out. From Egypt the onion entered Greece and on to Italy, thence into all of Europe."
Better Living Cookbook

When I think how far the onion has traveled
just to enter my stew today, I could kneel and praise
all small forgotten miracles,
crackly paper peeling on the drainboard,
pearly layers in smooth agreement,
the way knife enters onion
and onion falls apart on the chopping block,
a history revealed.

And I would never scold the onion
for causing tears.
It is right that tears fall
for something small and forgotten.
How at meal, we sit to eat,
commenting on texture of meat or herbal aroma
but never on the translucence of onion,
now limp, now divided,
or its traditionally honorable career:
For the sake of others,
disappear.

TWO COUNTRIES

Skin remembers how long the years grow
when skin is not touched, a gray tunnel
of singleness, feather lost from the tail
of a bird, swirling onto a step,
swept away by someone who never saw
it was a feather. Skin ate, walked,
slept by itself, knew how to raise a
See-you-later hand. But skin felt
it was never seen, never known as
a land on the map, nose like a city,
hip like a city, gleaming dome of the mosque
and the hundred corridors of cinnamon and rope.

Skin had hope, that's what skin does.
Heals over the scarred place, makes a road.
Love means you breathe in two countries.
And skin remembers—silk, spiny grass,
deep in the pocket that is skin's secret own.
Even now, when skin is not alone,
it remembers being alone and thanks something larger
that there are travelers, that people go places
larger than themselves.

A DEFINITE SHORE

"What is it that is wrecking our lives?"
Daud Kamal

The boy who ate poisoned fish in Sri Lanka covers his eyes.
Each time the plane shudders his knuckles whiten.
He wants to be home.

Below us the hungry Atlantic pushes and pulls
its waves across the earth.
All we want is to land safely again,

we who calculate our luckiness, who worry that the pocket
must be growing a hole. The bread seller of Aleppo
wanted only to sell his bread. And the Saudi women

who said, "Tell them we *are* oppressed, but *not* stupid,"
had just that message in mind.
We signed each others' notebooks as if

those addresses were a definite shore.
Once on a bus out of Nepal
I prayed for nothing but flat land.

It seemed so easy, being reduced
to a single wish! In those moments
I think our lives are laughing at us.

They know the moment a wish is answered
our hearts will open like sieves
and everything fall through again.

They know that women and men have been
wanting so much for so long
a flat highway will only remind us of heat,

of sleeping, the deliberate stones
crossing this season, the arrogant river
tumbling beneath.

43

TELLING THE STORY

In America, what's real
juggles with what isn't:
a woman I know props fabulous tulips
in her flowerbed, in snow.

Streets aren't gold, but they could be.
Once a traveler mailed letters
in a trashcan for a week.
He thought they were going somewhere.
In America everything is going somewhere.

I answered a telephone
on a California street.
Hello? It was possible.
A voice said, "There is no scientific proof
that God is a man."
"Thank you." I was standing there.
Was this meant for me?
It was not exactly the question
I had been asking, but it kept me busy awhile,
telling the story.

Some start out
with a big story
that shrinks.

Some stories accumulate power
like a sky gathering clouds,
quietly, quietly,
till the story rains around you.

Some get tired of the same story
and quit speaking;
a farmer leaning into
his row of potatoes,
a mother walking the same child
to school.
What will we learn today?
There should be an answer,
and it should
change.

AT MOTHER TERESA'S

Finally there are enough people to hug!
A room of 2-year-olds with raised arms. . .
we swing them into the air,
their grins are windows
in a city of crumbling walls.
One girl stays in the corner
crouched over her shoes.
Hard to keep shoes in this world,
people steal them, they walk away.
Her flaming hair is a house
she lives in all alone.
When I touch it she looks up,
suspicious, then lifts
a stub of chalk from her shoe.
Makes 3 jagged lines on the floor.
Can I read? I nod rapidly,
imagining *love me, love me, yes,*
but she is too alone to believe it.
Her face closes. I will never guess.

Calcutta, 1984

THE ENDLESS INDIAN NIGHTS

How the same Shah who commanded thousands
to build the Taj Mahal could later be jailed for life
by a single son is something to think about
during the endless Indian nights.
In the stump of candle,
a crooked wick keeps sinking.
I press my lips to your back.
All night the tiresome anklet of charms and voices:
no no no, three times, the way they say in Asia,
or the Goan priest who wrote a farewell letter in couplets.
He even spoke in rhyme and could rhyme with Ghandi.
On the table our tea was deep, and true.

Everywhere camels plunge to their knees
and pretend there are no people.
A villager asked me, "What is your caste?"
"We don't have castes in America." He stared harder.
"Then how do you know who you are?"

Tonight I would laugh less,
I would place my hands together and ask
how he sleeps in this populous dark.
On the boulevard from earth to moon
our wings are dragging.
The babies of Calcutta, bearers with empty baskets,
sorrowful fringe of the robe—how many times
do we put you on? It was dark, then it was dark again.
It was dark so long we thought the day was lost.
I lay thinking of Afghanistan, men who live in caves
eating potatoes till their faces grow longer,
their eyes blacken and will not close.
Someone said the world has never forgotten anyone
better. And I vowed to remember them

though what good it would do, who knows.
At dawn a cook wept in the kitchen,
once he cooked for Maharajah and now he cooked for pigs.
I thanked him so many times for his omelette.
He wanted letters from America saying
he was a good cook. I promised,
the morning unwrapped its shining turban
and flung it wide, so we dreamed we were done
with sleeping. It reached a new momentum,
like a professor who keeps writing onto the wall
after he fills the blackboard and the students,
startled, pay better attention. *What is this?*
Because now that there are no borders
they could imagine him continuing onto their desks,
their innocent skin.

NEWS TRAVELING WELL

In south India,
Vimala strings mango leaves
above her door,
their brownness flutters
for months.
Each morning
she chalks a new mandala
on the sidewalk
so the gods will look down
and know everything is alright.
She rises early
to sweep away twigs which keep mounding
in small heaps
at her doorstep.
Her father planted
a fig tree.
By the time it bore fruit,
she was carrying his ashes home
from the crematorium.
What does this look like
from above?

Each message, each network of tears—
the peanut vendors
were fanning their smudge pots,
measuring smoky cones of nuts.
Indira's head fluttered
from a thousand city walls.
Overnight the posters grew ragged.
"No!" I yelled at a taxi,
but he followed me
for seven blocks.
The bullet that killed Mahatma Ghandi

is preserved under glass,
near spectacles, rice bowl,
and walking cane,
on red-stained cloth:
"WHAT TOOK BAPU AWAY FROM US."
Then the EXIT door,
so you carry it out
in your mind.

Maybe this is why
some people make shrines
in their kitchens,
incense and candles
smoldering all day, a dam against
the flood of news.
Why we step outside
after talking,
ashamed of our neat voices,
to feel wind,
the one complete sentence,
saying what we keep trying
to fold together.
Why the sleeper presses
his ear to the ground.

NO ONE THINKS OF TEGUCIGALPA

No one thinks of Tegucigalpa, unless you are the man
at the Christmas party who sells weapons to Honduras
and smilingly bets on war. Or you have been there,
you wear the miles of markets, a cascading undergarment
beneath your calm white shirt, the slick black tiles
of the plaza, a girl coming early, little hum and bucket,
to polish them. Near the river, a toothless man kept
parrots and monkeys in his yard. ¿ Por que? He said, "Love."

They don't want to hear about Tegucigalpa because it makes
them feel like a catalogue of omissions. Where is it?
Now who? As if Houston were everything, the sun comes up
because commerce exists . . . But if you kept driving south,
past Mexico's pointed peaks, the grieving villages of
Guatemala, you would reach the city that climbs hills,
opening its pink-lidded eye while the Peace Monument
draws a quiet breath. A boy stands all day skewering
lean squares of beef till the night hisses on his grill.

Where is it? At the end of the arm, so close I tap the
red roofs with my finger, the basket seller weaves a
crib for my heart. Think of the countries you have never
seen, the cities of those countries, start here, then ask:
How bad is it to dress in a cold room? How small your own
wish for a parcel of children? How remarkably invisible
this tear?

TILL NOW

I hid my lies behind the door where no one
would find them. If someone asked
What are you doing? I answered, Building
a castle. You can't see it but
I can see it. The truth is
I could never see it.

Beyond the walls and windows
the cherry trees were nets of fruit.
We held the pits on our tongues,
sliding them back and forth,
spitting into the iris. One night
bats hovered in a trembling cloud
above the house. I could see they
were not birds, but by then
no one believed.

Jealous of men who drive trucks,
who have straight destinations,
jealous of the farmer who is intimate
with furrow and wind, I lay down
my pride before him. Tell me
your secret, and his eyes widen.
I always wanted to be a singer, he confides.

Morning, shiny shoe, what do I do
to deserve you? I would say one word
to earn my breath. Steps of the church
alive with sun! A woman in black lace mantilla
eating a two-tone ice cream cone
for breakfast.

San Cristobal de Las Casas

51

WHAT IS GIVEN, WHAT IS NOT GIVEN

"Not sadness, which is always there. . ."
Phillip Lopate

To market, you hens with stunned faces,
crate of papaya, peanuts and corn.
Cart wheels fit the ruts in the road.
I stand back, a shadow.
Men who know each other are saying Good Day.
All my life I wanted to find the simplest
cleanest way of doing anything.
Something to plant in the heart—
a belief, a grove of trees.
Lost in the city of blue doors,
cloud cap on the mountain,
why should anyone nod?
Inside each memory shadows are the shrine.

On Chiapa de Corzo women line up for tortillas,
their faces soft with peace.
Maybe we read each other wrong.
Time which never fits the face I give it,
which always seems too short or too long,
how do I become your servant now?
My basket is small, it fits one finger.
After the market, mounds of withered leaves.

When will legs equal the streets
strung out before them?
Each year I listen harder
to hear it, corners whispering
Don't worry you will grow.

HER WAY

"He only listened to his own secret bell, ringing,
and saw another winter come."
Mahmud Darwish

What water she poured on the floor
was more than was needed. Someone suggested
she mop in strips as they did
on the television, yet her buckets were full,
the great buckets of field and orchard,
she was dragging them room to room
in a house that already looked clean.

The tune she hummed was nobody's tongue.
Already she had seen the brothers go off
in airplanes, she did not like the sound.
Skies opened and took people in.
The tune was long and had one line.

And the soldiers flipping I.D. cards,
the men who editorialized blood
till it was pale and not worth spilling,
meant nothing to her.
She was a woman shopping for fabric.
She was walking with her neck straight,
her eyes placed ahead.
What oil she rubbed on the scalp was pure.
The children she spoke to were news,
were listening, had names
and a scraped place on the elbow.
She could place a child in a bucket
and bathe it, could stitch the mouth
in the red shirt closed.

PAKISTAN WITH OPEN ARMS

Tonight in Karachi, a man drapes
jasmine garlands over his wrist
and looks both ways.
It is the hour of the walk,
when men and women come slowly forth
from houses, kitchens,
their stride growing long and musical,
sky finally softening its grip.
Whatever they talked about in the day
stands back to let them pass.

In some languages, a voice asking
a question goes up at the end
and an answer slopes toward the sea.
Maybe now the turtles are stepping
from their nests at the beach,
the huge shrine of their eggs behind them.
Maybe the fabulous painted buses
are cooling their engines at the lot.

How could I have seen, twenty years ago,
a night when a string of fragrant flowers
would be all I desired?
In the peaked shadow of his house
a man reads a map on which deserts
and mountains are different colors.
Each province has its own woven rugs
and speckled red hats.
He wishes to walk in a hundred villages
where people he will never meet are walking.

Into my arms I gather the quiet avenue,
the patience of curbs.
A family relaxes on a sweep of public grass.
Their shirts are cotton and silk.
They visit quietly as the moon comes speaking
its simple round name.
I gather them into me, saying,
This is the thunderous city.
This is the person who once was afraid.

WITH THE GREEKS

For Dan and Chrissie Anthony

When you dance Greek-style,
you wave a handkerchief,
the foot stomps, a necklace of islands
rises in the blood.
Moving through days,
the shadow of this circle
stays with you.
Outline of a wheeling fish
that says you are less alone
than you like to think.

At the grill, shrimp curl perfectly
on sticks. A sleek woman with a bow tie
strokes her husband's hand.
What have we in common?
Grandmother spooning honey-puffs
smiles at anyone, Here child, eat,
fortify yourself for the journey
between homes.

Floating heart, who knows
which hand is on which arm?
Whether any story begins or ends
where we say it does
or goes on like a circle,
common sea between stones and lamps.
In the villages of Greece,
windows light up, eyes.
Children carry things in baskets.
A basket sits on a floor.

I heard of an orchard where statues grew up
between the roots of trees. Stones were men,
one trunk had feet. I heard of an island
where snails rose from the dirt
and saved the people, who were starving.

Tonight there is no ocean
that does not sing. Even sorrow,
which we have felt and felt again
in all our lands, has hands.

WRITERS' CONFERENCE

No skyline is visible from
the Skyline Room yet we who place
so much faith in words ignore this.

Four ladies in the poetry workshop
do not write poetry, but like it.
If I talked about what I like,
they might leave. Writers confer
because they want a day off from writing.

This morning, blankly, I tried
to put on thoughts like clothes.

Writers need to give each other
picture postcards of mountains
pushing up through fog.
I found one once, at a Chinese junk store.
Mr. Wong said I could have it
if I took the whole bunch,
five pounds of cards, ten dollars.
But I only want one, I said.
This one.
He shrugged. He'd lived long enough
to know when someone really wants something.
I didn't have ten dollars, but that fog
kept getting more and more important.

Today we lean over lines, bird-tracks.
Who has seen this thing in the air?
Not I, says one. I deal more in the earthbound.
We juggle awhile and fold our papers
so they open out like roses.
Give us something we can use,
eyeglasses or ink!
Something definite, like a mountain.
Or the way Mr. Wong stops a moment
before locking his door and turns slowly,
feeling the huge presence of objects,
the dark breathing of fringes and bowls,
before he steps out into the street of his life
with empty hands.

LEO

The man can fish. Trout come to him,
flies to a fruit bar. The man stands
on the end of a pier at the end of a week
that meant nothing to him.
This is the way he closes the door.

While families sleep, he reels them in.
Moonlit backs, the thousand lights of a city
floating across the bay.

Somewhere behind him, black water has a mouth,
and is speaking. He is a boy learning
the questions which will come to him,
be put and put again, eyes baiting eyes
on a long line that never clicks.

If he knew how to keep walking out
toward morning across the black sea,
how to wake in a place where silence
is acceptable as sunlight speckling
the arms of trees and men, he would do it.
But the pier ends here, and so he stands.
Tomorrow they will ask, "Any luck?"
and he will look in his bucket to know.

WHERE THE SOFT AIR LIVES

"Meanwhile Dean and I went out to dig the streets of Mexican San Antonio.
It was fragrant and soft—the softest air I'd ever known—and dark, and
mysterious, and buzzing. Sudden figures of girls in white bandannas
appeared in the humming dark."
Jack Kerouac, *On the Road*

1.

She placed her babies in the sink
stroking off the heat with an old damp rag.
Coo-coo little birdies, she sang,
then she tied the hair up in ponytails
pointing to the moon. It made them look
like little fruits with a pointed end.
She said, You don't think about poverty
till someone comes over.

2.

The man on Guadalupe Street is
guarding the cars. On his porch
the lights of Virgin Mary flash
endlessly, prayer-time, vigilante,
he rocks with his wife every night
rocking, while the bakery seals its cases
of pumpkin tart and the boys
with T-shirts slashed off below the nipples
strut big as buses past his gate.
He is keeping an eye on them.
And on fenders, hubcaps,
a grocery cart let loose
and lodged against a fence.
Cars roar past, but they will have
to go home again. He is happy
in this life, blinking Mother of God,
his wife placing one curl of mint in the tea,
saying always the same line,
Is it sweet enough? and the porch
painted three shades of green.

3.

I mended my ways, he said.
I took a needle and big thread and mended them.
You would not know me to see me now.
Sometimes I see myself sweeping the yard,
watering the dog, and I think
who is that guy? He looks like an old guy.
He looks like a guy who tells you
fifteen dead stories and mixes them up.
So that explains it:
why I don't tell you nuthin.

4.

She feeds her roses coffee
to make them huge. When her son was in Vietnam
the bougainvillea turned black once overnight.
But he didn't die. She prescribes lemongrass,
manzanilla: in her album the grandchildren
smile like seed packets.
She raises the American flag on her pole
because she is her own Mexican flag
and the wind fluttering the hem of her dress
says there is no border in the sky.

5.

Lisa's husband left, so she dyed her hair
a different color every day. Once pale silk,
next morning, a flame. She shaped her nails,
wore a nightgown cut down so low
the great canyon between her bosoms
woke up the mailman dragging his bag.

She pulled the bed into the dining room,
placed it dead center, never went out.
TV, eyelash glue, pools of perfume.
She was waiting for the plumber,

the man who sprays the bugs. Waiting
to pay a newspaper bill, to open her arms,
unroll all her front pages
and the sad unread sections too,
the ads for bacon and cleanser,
the way they try to get you to come to the store
by doubling your coupons,
the way they line the ads in red.

6.

Air filled with hearts,
we pin them to our tongues,
follow the soft air back to its cave
between trees, river of air
pouring warm speech, two-colored speech
into the streets. *Make a house
and live in it.*

At the Mission Espada
the priest keeps a little goat
tied to a stump.
His people come slowly out
of the stone-white room,
come lifting their feet suddenly heavy,
trying to remember far back before
anything had happened twice.
Someone lit a candle, and it caught.
A girl in a white dress,
singing in a window.
And you were getting married,
getting born, seeing the slice of blue
that meant *shore;*
the goat rises,
his bitten patch of land around him.
The priest bends to touch his head.
And goes off somewhere.
But the air behind him
still holding that hand, and the little goat
still standing.

A HOUSE WITH NO ONE IN IT

Each time you drive away
I drop into the cave where
26 million bats spend the summer.
I comb my silken pouch
of voices: your voice
at the top of the stairs,
your voice on waking,
the soft slur of dreaming
still damp on its edge.

West of here, deserts
are pooling their silences.
I pack my bag
but each shirt is a stone.
Tonight I will keep track
of something,
words to say upon your return.

And the bats whom so few people
have ever loved go in and out
their limestone walls,
gathering mosquitoes
into warm bellies,
holding themselves in the
swelling dark.

PABLO AND I HAVE LUNCH

Yesterday I felt comfortable
with my life of chicken coops.
A possum came to visit: this was news.
Today you list filmmakers, dancers, writers,
quick foreign names. I have nothing to say.
You attack whole armies of thought
with a single spear and win.
Now you are telling me what to order,
sneering at pickles, raising your hand
like a priest over this shabby world.
Listen brother, I like my city.
I am getting older. This is not news.
The years between our sandwiches
have been slopes, gradual as New England.
Remember when we stood arm-in-arm
on the last day of the year, burning mail?
I live like that smoke.
I live like that poof and hiss, I stock up nothing.
This agenda you give me, this urgent demand
that I "branch out" is the last door
closing between us.
We are the twins
who did not live like mirrors.

On the way to the car we pass
Julio's Shoe Repair Shop,
scuffed heels piled like junk.
Julio hammers in the belly of the store.
He saw two miracles once.
I think you should be his apprentice,
learn to hold nails in your mouth.
And I want to ask him what goes through his head,
holding this thing of leather, this very simple thing
that has walked so far
for somebody else.

RAIN

A teacher asked Paul
what he would remember
from third grade, and he sat
a long time before writing
"this year sumbody tutched me
on the sholder"
and turned his paper in.
Later she showed it to me
as an example of her wasted life.
The words he wrote were large
as houses in a landscape.
He wanted to go inside them
and live, he could fill in
the windows of "o" and "d"
and be safe while outside
birds building nests in drainpipes
knew nothing of the coming rain.

THE MAN WHO HATED TREES

When he started blaming robberies
on trees, you knew for sure
something was wrong.

This man who clipped hair,
who spent years shaving the necks
of cafeteria managers,
sweeping lost curls down drains,
this man who said, "It is always better
to cut off a little too much. . ."

You could say he transferred
one thing to another when he came home,
hair to leaves, only this time
he was cutting down whole bodies,
from the feet up, he wanted
to make those customers stumps.

One tree dropped purple balls
on the roof of his car.
One tree touched the rain gutter.
He didn't like blossoms, too much mess.
"Trees take up the sky.
It's my light, why share it?"
He said thieves struck more
on blocks where there were trees.
"The shade, you know. They like the dark."
You lived for days with the buzz of his chain saw
searing off the last little branches of neighborly affection.

It was planting season in the rest of the town
but your street received a crew cut.
Two pecan trees that had taken half a century to rise

now stood like Mohawk Indians, shorn.
He gloated on his porch surrounded by amputations.
You caught him staring greedily
at the loose branches swinging over your roof.

Tomorrow, when everything was cut, what then?
He joked about running over cats
as the last chinaberry crashed,
as the truck came to gather arms and legs
waggling their last farewell.

What stories did he tell himself,
this patriot of springtime,
and how did it feel to drive down sprouting boulevards
with his bald, bald heart?

FOR LUKE, LEAVING US

I'll remind you how we broke sticks
to cook breakfast if you can tell me
the thing that raises you up.
I want the hope that finds us
in closets, stuffs our smallest
aching bone.
I want to find you the way
you found me, lost, on Old Baldy,
your voice letting out its strings,
pulling me in.

Magazines seem foolish as I hand them over.
You say you are following maps,
blue line that was Utah wraps twice
around your head, lifts you back
toward somewhere.
We ate corn soup in bowls made of clay.
Once we walked without clothes a whole mile
and no one saw us.

Dinner is quick, bland, has nothing to chew.
A sign says, "NEXT MEAL, BREAKFAST.
NEXT HOLIDAY, CHRISTMAS."
They talk to you as if an hour still has sides.

You remember the man who ran the motel in Flagstaff
that winter you were snowed in.
You wake reciting his recipe for eggs.

Across the hall, a man pleads for a bedpan
in Spanish. *I hate him,* you say.
And cover your face, hating everything.
On the elevator I weep for every button.

One week you are calm and planning.
You wear your flannel bathrobe tied.
One week you swear you will return

to Thoreau, New Mexico,
and camp on the red road.
A whisper, "I am depressed," and the window shade
stays closed, stays closed.

Now the friends find themselves
cursing food carts with neat stacked trays.
Nothing should be neat.
Each morning rings with your face.
Who are we to be living it up
in a world where no one saves anyone?
So we loved you, it is no ladder.
You sink deeper and deeper,
no arm is long enough to reach you.

I want to say how we are reaching
even after you go,
you color the days like a purple shadow
saying you were not finished,
Montana is a big state.

YOU HAVE TO BE CAREFUL

You have to be careful telling things.
Some ears are tunnels.
Your words will go in and get lost in the dark.
Some ears are flat pans like the miners used
looking for gold.
What you say will be washed out with the stones.

You look a long time till you find the right ears.
Till then, there are birds and lamps to be spoken to,
a patient cloth rubbing shine in circles,
and the slow, gradually growing possibility
that when you find such ears,
they already know.

OVER THE FENCE

It is no miracle, she says.
A husband drives away,
the world clicks shut
like a little dead door.
If I could go to a movie
that lasted longer than my life
it might be alright.

I was born on this street,
the man who shot himself in your bathroom
was my first friend.
My mother closed the shades
when the ambulance came.
A dish is dirty, is clean, is dirty,
what song is this if
it's the only one you know?

Don't tell the trashmen
I'm here alone.
Tell them we're late sleepers,
the curtains stay shut
so we can live like kings.

On your side of the fence
iris float their silken heads.
Over here the rose is a stick forever.

You say I'm lucky to know
two languages. What good are two words
if no one can hear them?
I'd take one tongue if it fit me,
I'd wear it like the postman
wears his suit, so people know
what he is doing in the world.
Walk up and down the street
delivering smiles.
I say no one is lucky.
We have faces, they get old.

HAWAIIAN PUNCH PRAYER, AUGUST

They pound on my door so long
I have to open it.
He asks if I'm sick,
if anyone in my house is sick.
"A man of optimism!" I say.
He does not smile.
She holds a Hawaiian Punch can
with the label soaked off.

One hundred degrees—
some months should be sidestepped
like dogs in the street.

"Is your mother home?"
he asks with that fishy voice.
I think, Probably. Maybe.
She is home in her own home,
who can see across
three hundred miles?

He offers to sell me a prayer.
"Very cheap, you name the reason."

I think how 30 years ago
my mother placed me
in a cradle of prayers,
stood singing in the shadows
till I let go her hand.

There were prayers
lodged between the teeth
of nuns in Cuzco.
In Guatemala, children
whose parents had fallen

into the ground
touched our hair
and sang hymns.

And this is what I have come to?

Some days it looks like a long life
all up and down the street
with tired fans wheeling
and doors that only go shut.

FRENCH MOVIES

In memory of Patrick Dewaere

1.

Roasted chicken placed on a linen cloth.
In the movie it is still sitting there.
You forgot to eat it. We go outside to find
glass bottles smashed behind our cars.

2.

In some men the future is written
with a definite pen.
He strides out of here,
heading into the future.

You were a page of mist,
hovering. Your voice said
other people's words,
erased its own.

How they explained it:
He was fragile,
couldn't face reality.

One radiant tear in a train station—
even today, all our ages stand still
in your face. It is impossible
to blink.

3.

I wish I could have held on
to your coattails.
We could have stood with the other half-sure ones
near the lighthouse in the tourist town
listening to wave and cloud,

the way no script written there
survives, and who worries about it?
Then when they stood in line to say
this world was not enough, perhaps
you would not be among them.
Knowing that story already,
you could make a different one.
The French critic reminds us
the French like their movies ambiguous.

4.

Here in a country of real estate and sun,
you visit only briefly.
Materialize on the screen,
then whisk away,
leaving us pale shoulders,
slightly balding spot on the back of the skull,
maps to a country which no longer exists.
I wish your coattails had been longer.
If we are not fragile, we don't deserve the world.

WHO'S WHO, 1941

I'm being insulted in a library. The librarian thinks I'm a high
school student sneaking out of class. "Who do you think you are?"
she shouts. We are alone. I want to answer enigmatically. I am the
ghost pressing against your window. I am the termite feasting on the
secret boards of your house. She stands, she glares at me. She has a
hairdo. The rest of the school is taking a test.

Some say everything is taken from us. A bowl is carried to the sink,
wiped clean. It does not remember who ate from it. Still we have
these moments when we remember what we never knew. A picture in
an old reference book looms familiar as a mother, a life story told in
neat clipped sentences is the life you might be living right now, in
the thin white space between lines. Will this be the year you do
something you remember?

"I am not a student," I say. I speak too clearly, like a translator.
"I am a student, but not the kind you think." She glares. It is
possible she truly hates me. And I place the book back on her shelf
as if it were a real book, as if those people pictured in the gray and
white 1940's photographs accompany me at all times, book or no.
Then I go trembling out into a world of rain, looking for them.

CATALOGUE ARMY

Something has happened to my name.
It now appears on catalogues
for towels and hiking equipment,
dresses spun in India,
hand-colored prints of parrots and eggs.
Fifty tulips are on their way
if I will open the door.
Dishrags from North Carolina
unstack themselves in the Smoky Mountains
and make a beeline for my sink.

I write a postcard to my cousin:
this is what it is like to live in America.
Individual tartlet pans congregate
in the kitchen, chiming my name.
Porcelain fruit boxes float above tables,
sterling silver ice cream cone holders
twirl upside down on the cat's dozing head.

For years I developed radar against malls.
So what is it that secretly applauds
this army of catalogues marching upon my house?
I could be in the bosom of poverty, still they arrive.
I could be dead, picked apart by vultures,
still they would tell me
what socks to wear in my climbing boots.

Stay true, catalogues, protect me
from the wasteland where whimsy and impulse
never camp.
Be my companion on this journey between dusts,
between vacancy and that smiling stare
that is citizen of every climate
but customer to nothing,
even air.

SOME RELIEF TO THINK OF STARS

The casual inquiry—where is he?
to be answered only by, He is everywhere
or, He is dead, suspends the tongue.
After this there are no other places
for awhile, no lights in the field
to signify cotton gin or gas pump or cafe.

Once I stood with horses till
in near darkness a horse leaned its bulk
away from me and breathed out heavily
against the stall's metal rungs.
Such a complete outpouring of breath,
it came from all the corners of a horse,
bending knee, curve from neck to face,
each slick and pebbled ridge.
I wanted to copy him, losing
my quiet knowing voice
and the high hysterical tone,
dropping them out in one vast
exultant heave. Deep above us
stars washed the sky.
Stars waving their milky brooms
saying whatever we couldn't do
they would do in our places—
it is always some relief
to think of stars.

Now you are with them, choosing it,
which makes all the difference,
leaving stones and trees and envelopes,
girls in ruffled party dresses,
even party dresses, which you loved!
And we who knew so much
did not know this:
that you could close that door so hard.

The door is wood.
The hinge is soft, and sobbing.
All night, voices enter,
each spilling a different story
you would have saved:
the green bean truck in Sudan, Texas,
which bumped over 3 sets of railroad tracks
without losing a single bean.

A man who raised canaries in his barn,
painstakingly measuring handfuls of seed
into rows of tiny cups. . .
what else was he good for?
The birds were jumping from one leg
to another. He could no longer say
where his hobby began.

WHAT HE SAID TO HIS ENEMIES

He could hear them off in the forest,
massive branches breaking:
you are no good, will never be any good.

Sometimes they followed him,
rubbing out his tracks.
They wanted him to get lost
in the world of trees,
stand silently forever, holding up his hands.

At night he watched
the streetlamp's light
soaking into his lawn.
He could bathe in its cool voice,
roll over to a whole different view.
What made them think
the world's room was so small?

On the table he laid out his clothes,
arranging the cuffs.
What he said to his enemies
was a window pushed high as it would go.
Come in, look for me where you think
I am. Then when you see no one is there,
we can talk.

WOOD

The silence of a desk
is good to return to
after conversation with human beings
where sentences went up
and some went down.

The drawers in a desk
are smaller than the drawers of the heart
but more predictable.
If you place something here,
it will be waiting when you get back.

Hard to imagine the heart being so plain,
holding no more than what it is given
when all around the earth stretches out
its giant fields.

The heart coasts through fields, gathering.
The heart comes and goes like a crow.

While the desk waits in the room
where light and dark revolve so quietly
it is as if nothing happens, as if
the shadow sleeping inside the wood
slides out for a few hours
and folds in again, still empty.

As if the papers with words on them
were written by wood that, slowly,
would last that long.

ROPES

On the beach at Karachi, a man tells his monkey
to dance, to strut like Nehru, to bounce on his hands.
Behind us a camel pauses: it has just walked
six miles without a rope.
Tonight its owner will step outside
and become hysterical. But the rope
on Mister Potato's neck is firm.
He crosses his legs carefully,
placing huge sunglasses over his nose.
He beats a drum and swivels his head.
The terrified gaze says:
It is not happily a monkey does these things.

From the waves, women race, wringing their dripping
shalwar kameez. To be barer? Unthinkable.
They detest the foolishness a beach attracts,
magicians, snake charmers with exhausted mongoose
and swollen flutes. After hours of their music
it sounds like a movie where everyone goes mad.
We see best what we have never seen before;
horizon over this repetitive little act.
The man with the monkey sets it moving,
then looks away.

Yesterday at the airport in Dubai,
Pakistani laborers crouched together near the gate.
"You will rise!" shouted a hostess.
"You will please to sit in your seats!"
They crouched unmoving, nooses of smoke
sliding from their cigarettes.
A very old white-bearded one smiled so hard
you knew he knew what was going on.
The men had been heaving crates for months,

fingering their tight passports,
sleeping in the butchers' alley near the canal.
Now they were going home with their envelopes
and they wanted to sit on the floor.

For a moment the monkey is just a monkey.
You want to hold him there, where four paws
touched ground and stricken eyes darted,
where the leash went suddenly slack.
Down the beach the nuclear power plant
casts its vaulted shadow over the waves.

Tonight you will learn Afghanistan has no seacoast.
A man will show where a shark once bit him open,
jagged seam across his thigh.
A magician will say he would be rich by now
had he only stayed in Hong Kong performing for businessmen
who know how wonderful it is to spring free from a rope
after tying it very tightly around your own neck,
letting everyone check it to be sure.

GRATEFUL

From the stick that is my head,
I carve a new head, one to be used
for walking. Clear the path
of all debris.

I tip the bucket of my heart
and empty it. It fills immediately.
Inside, you are shining,
all the men and women are shining.
I take the bucket and kiss
the arc of its handle.

To the sinking ship of memory,
be my guest, drop what you have
to the bottom. Myriad ladders
of blue, strange shapely tails
of fish, to the blind cave.
Up here sky is the lasting country.

I take the future paved with advice,
turning it over and over like
a document or ironed tablecloth.
Whole days go by, it seems
nothing has moved.
Still our birthdays chug toward us
irreverently. What new knowledge
will we bring to the station?
Once when an airplane almost crashed
but didn't, we said, "This is it.
I will be grateful for the rest of my life."

Some days any corner is a home.
For once the thin criminal on the bicycle
says nothing ugly, but nods.
I will think of him differently.
I take the old thinking and bury it.
Take the scarred wheel,
brush dipped in yellow paint.
I take this window
I have been sitting in front of
and look through it.
Birds we will never touch
are flying away.

WHEN THE FLAG IS RAISED

For Judith McPheron

Today the vein of sadness pumps
its blue wisdom through this room and
you answer with curtains. A curtain lifts
and holds itself aloft.

Somewhere in Texas, a motel advertises
rooms for "A Day, Week, Month, or Forever."
The melancholia of this invitation
dogs me for miles.
Sometimes I lie in bed reading biographies,
traveling one paragraph three times
to feel its graceful turns and glides.
Naturally all other lives feel
more solid and trustworthy
than any life right in front of me
which is the great stupidness
of my kind of animal.
Nothing is ever the same because
no one else is either.
I go to the sink, splash water on my face.
In the morning sailors in sailor suits
park their cars in front of my house
and march around the block.
It's as if we live on different shores.

More than anything I honor how some voices
raise a flag, even if the sinking country
will not stay whole. When we reconsider
our own vanishing measures of air,

84

when the great loser of the heart
subtracts another odyssey, stitching itself
a new garment of pink skin,
the flag is above us, waving without urgency,
waving like the word "remember"
triggers the tongue.

I will remember how I woke with your voice
filtering other voices, steadily penetrating
the walls, saying, Traveler, saying, Take Note,
so I was packing the small bag from the beginning again
as if anyone could use it.
Now it was breath and needle,
the impeccable fine print of leaves.
We were leaving the grip of silence behind us.
There were so many people we needed to see.